Happy Christmas 2010

As you like thought you might enjoy this book

KU-175-756

Shakespeare In a Nutshell

Timothy Robey

Bright Pen

Visit us online at www.authorsonline.co.uk

A Bright Pen Book

Text Copyright © Timothy Robey 2009

Additional Illustrations by © Jo Spaul

Cover design by Jo Spaul & Jamie Day ©

ISBN 978 07552 1178 4

Authors OnLine Ltd
19 The Cinques
Gamlingay, Sandy
Bedfordshire SG19 3NU
England

This book is also available in e-book format, details of which are available at www.authorsonline.co.uk

ABOUT THE AUTHOR

Timothy Robey's first love was chemistry. He graduated from Imperial College, became a Chartered Chemist and taught the subject for many years.

It was a school production of *Richard II* that first aroused his interest in Shakespeare - an interest which has deepened steadily, as he has found that life experience intensifies one's appreciation of the dramatist's understanding of human character.

Timothy has been writing verse for many years and has published several books of poems. Some of these include an unusual 'quiz' element - an indirect consequence of his participation in *Mastermind* and *15 to 1*, and this characteristic features in *Shakespeare in a Nutshell*. Modern expressions and anachronisms, such as Gene Pool *(Romeo and Juliet)*, Retirement Arrangements *(King Lear)*, and Credit Crunch *(The Merchant of Venice)* may amuse, and perhaps alert us to the timelessness of Shakespeare's themes.

H.R.

A WORD FROM THE AUTHOR

Some readers who love Shakespeare may be horrified by the liberties I have taken. Others may take a more relaxed approach, and perhaps even feel that Shakespeare himself might have been amused. I like to think that a few may find their understanding of Shakespeare enhanced.

This book is dedicated to my wife, Helen, who has helped me in many ways.

Many thanks to www.JoSpaul.co.uk, who has shown imagination and great care in the art work.

CONTENTS

The Tragedies

The Comedies

The Histories and the Roman Plays

QQQQ

The Real Thing

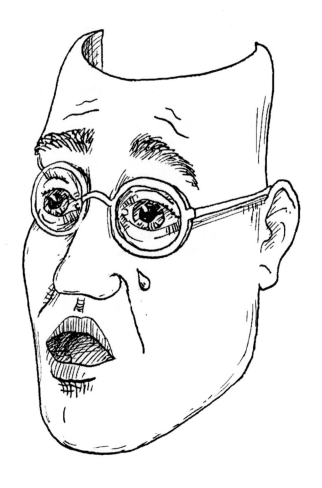

The Tragedies

MACBETH

Macbeth and Banquo thought that they
Had served their King in every way,
And so they could not understand
The tame succession Duncan planned.

Upon a twisted, blasted heath —
Their fancies steeped in bas-relief —
They thought they saw those skinny crones
Concocting broth from eyes and bones.

The crones, of course, did not exist
But Macbeth's mind could not resist
The thought of being Scotland's king —
There lay the witches' spited sting.

Macbeth had long been Thane of Glamis,
A post which held restricted charms,
But when ennobled once again,
The witches' promise seemed quite plain.

The weakened man strove to be true:
He is our King — a good one too;
His lady's weave was Chuckling thin —
'When he's our guest, we'll do him in.'

A dagger hovered near his hand
Just as the witches' guile had planned.
Wife-goading that he was no man
Was just a link in Evil's plan.

The dying Duncan glimpsed a friend
As spurting gore enguled his end,
As blood smeared on a sleeping groom
Ensured *his* guilt and strangled doom.

The ill-crowned King lived smudged in fear
That ending of his life was near —
For Banquo might produce a line
Of monarchs mirrored-out in time.

Poetic ruffians were hired,
No doubt in darkened cloaks attired,
But still Macbeth slept steeped in doubt
Since Banquo's son escaped the rout.

A rotting lingered in his mind,
A fruit that festers in its rind,
And yet he countered fear with scorn —
Macduff was of *some* woman born —

And all seemed better now he knew
How well the trees at Birnam grew:
To all and sundry it was plain
They'd never come to Dunsinane.

His Lady tried to wash away
Those crimson-blacks of yesterday,
But doctors could prescribe no cure
Because her guilt was spliced to fear.

The woods *did* move,
And very soon
Untimely-ripped-from-mother's-womb
The Thane of Fife — His Children Dead —
Took claim of a once-honest head.

The head was severed — that is true —
Yes — this is still what men may do.
But trees stay rooted where they grow;
It's fear that makes it seem not so.

RETIREMENT ARRANGEMENTS

King Lear decided in old age
His life had reached retirement stage,
So he would split his realm in three
And thought his daughters would agree;
He hoped that this might well be best —
Like Gaul of old, divisum est.

Two daughters, Goneril and Reg.,
Bestowed on him a fulsome pledge
That all their love was for their Dad —
Which made Cordelia screaming mad:
How could, this youngest daughter said,
They say such things when they were wed?

Those lady dogs! how could they dare
Deny their husbands proper care?
When *she* was joined they heard her say,
She'd know where love and duty lay.
Her honesty brought no reward —
The sneering King thought her a fraud.

The Duke of Burgundy had sought
Cordelia's hand, but judged she ought
Entitle him to be the heir
To what he thought was his fair share.
When his request earned old Lear's frown
Fine Burgundy got watered down.

Cordelia's land was given to
Those hypocrites, the other two.
The Earl of Kent opined 'Unfair',
So he was banished then and there;
Though France, to his eternal fame,
Let good Cordelia take his name.

But where was Lear himself to go —
He'd alternate between them so
Each daughter whom he thought a pearl
Could be his Daddy-loving girl.
His wiser Fool did not mistake
Twinned pitfalls in the path he'd take.

For those who read this savage play,
So black, so white, so rarely grey,
If overwhelmed, this couplet writ
May well, for some, increase their wit:
As hand fits in alternate glove,
So flattery misfits with love.

GLOUCESTER

With a chip upon his shoulder,
With a mountain on his back,
Gloucester's lust for Crown and glory
Drives him down his murderous track.

AFTERTHOUGHT

Macbeth, of course, could never know
Descendants of dispatched Banquo
Gave ancestry to that royal breed
To which Prince Charles may soon succeed.

CYMBELINE

King Cymbeline had always planned
To give his daughter's precious hand
To step-son Cloten, since he thought
That this would unify his court.

In secret Imogen had wed
A good, but foolish, lord instead,
Since, being careful and astute,
She judged that Cloten was a brute.

The Groom, when banished, went to Rome,
While Imogen was kept at home,
Since Leonatus Posthumus
Though kind was impecunious.

Alas, this man was sadly tricked
In thinking that his wife had slipped
And this so persecutes his life
He orders her to face the knife.

The faithful Imogen survives
In several miscellaneous lives,
And even earns an honest wage
By serving as a general's page.

And then, if you believe such tales,
Found living in a cave in Wales
The King's lost sons are rediscovered
And are restored to be step-mothered.

Fair Gentles, shun this nasty play,
(Too like the ones they write today).
'Beheaded, dressed in husband's clothes'
May well disturb your sweet repose:
For once you've seen dismembered Cloten
The sight can never be forgotten.

LADIES

'Julius dear,' said his good lady,
'Crowns of course are just for show,
But that meeting at the Senate —
P'r'aps it would be wise to go.'

'Fight for France,' saints seemed to tell her;
'See the Dauphin crowned at Rheims.'
La Pucelle, the flame of freedom
Will not be all that it seems.

'Thane of Cawdor,' soothed his lady,
'Being small my wants are few,
But to please your dainty wifeling
Knife the King — and Banquo too!'

'When she has no meat to feed on
And scant clothes upon her back,
Sun and Man are Moon and Maiden
As Kath'rina changes track.

'Cleo,' sighed a saddened Tony,
'You have caused me great distress;
First we lost our naval battle,
Then that asp went down your dress!'

'Hark!' the Bard said to his lady
'Owls behoot the twilight gloom —
A merry note — tu-whit, tu-who.'
'William, Dear, it should be whom.'

TIMON

A man of wealth, good Timon would help all:
He paid to have a prisoned friend released;
He gave a servant crowns so he could wed —
While gold remained his bounty never ceased.

His steward, Flavius, had tried to warn
How quickly even mighty fortunes fall:
His feasts and lavish gifts would very soon
Consume his lands, his bonds, his very all.

As creditors flocked to his open door
He sent to friends to help him in his need,
But as the orchid fades within the hour
Sun-flowering friends had quickly run to seed.

A misanthrope now living in a cave,
He digs for roots and finds a hoard of gold —
So scrounging flatterers at length return
To refit in their comfy little mould.

But Flavius stays loyal, his servants too.
Transmuting gold, the sponging yellow wage,
Can make the fool seem wise, the wise a fool;
The prating wise, perhaps, but not the sage.

HAMLET

When Claudius and Gertrude heard
That Hamlet was at Wittenberg,
They killed the King and grabbed the Throne
Before our hero could get home.
(They murdered, later it's made clear,
By pouring poison in the ear).

As Hamlet was a decent lad
He listened to his ghostly Dad,
Especially as the pair had wed
And no doubt cuddled up in bed —
For then, perchance, the time might come
When rival princes graced Gert's tum.

After he through-the-arras stabbed
And found the Chamberlain kebabbed,
The wily King and Queen were glad
To have him certified as mad,
And sent to England where they say
That that's endemic anyway.

The admin. failed so that instead
It's R. and G. who lost their head,
And pirates helped the Prince return
Where there was dreadful news to learn:
His jilted orphaned girlfriend took
Her life by floating down the brook.

Gravedigger turned him out a skull
Which made the saddened Hamlet mull
Upon those days, now gone, alack,
When Yorick gave him piggy-back —
Oh, was that wise man such a fool
When Hamlet was at infant school?

Alas, throughout the play we find
That Hamlet often changed his mind,
Though now the Prince could not defer
The slaying of Dad's murderer;
In consequence I really ought
To cut this gruesome story short.

With venomed foil and poisoned cup,
Dramatis personae used up,
Our play draws to its tragic end
With almost no one on the mend —
Though William somehow does contrive
To keep Horatio alive.

MORE OF VENICE

'Desdemona,' warned Othello,
'Cassio's beyond repair —
All that Dogey hanky-panky
Only brings the Moor despair.'

'Othello,' snapped the young detective,
Flicking o'er a notebook leaf,
'Your complaints are insubstantial;
Based upon a handkerchief!'

GHOST STORY

First Marcellus and Bernado,
At their castle-guarding post,
Saw the spectre which they realized
Must be Hamlet's father's ghost.

Horatio, a friend of Hamlet,
Not convinced, and rational,
Seeing it dissolve at cock-crow
Thought he'd better tell his pal.

Hamlet went all quaint and sullen
After he had spoke with Dad —
Uncle was a rotten killer
And his Mum had wed the cad.

'Hamlet, dear,' his mother soothed him
'You have made a great mistake;
Surely Daddy wasn't murdered —
He was poisoned by a snake.'

'No,' laughed Yorick, when consulted,
'That was some malicious tongue.
Since you got that First at Uni
You have been all highly strung.'

H. and O. were to be married —
Banns were on their final call —
When a glowing Spectre uttered,
'Hamlet did not dream it all.'

TITUS

Andronicus had five-and-twenty sons,
But one-and-twenty died in war
Leaving him exactly four.

He slaughtered one for standing in his way.
Though promised this would not be done,
Two were beheaded, leaving one.

His daughter, cast off by the Emperor,
Was widowed, lost her hands and tongue,
Then stabbed — so back again to one.

His wife, oh surely there was more than one,
Producing infants by the score,
Might well have wondered just what for.

GENE POOL

'Hi Juliet, it would be cool
To double-up on our gene pool —
The Reverend Lawrence in his cell,
Thinks everything should augur well —
With Montague enriched with Capulet
What precious boon should fair Verona get.'

"My Mum and Dad want me to wed,
A prospect I most deeply dread,
A Count, who's young and good it's true,
But always solving sudoku —
Oh Romeo, how could I ever bear
To be the wife of such a boring square?"

'O Juliet, my suit is true —
My chromosomes are right for you —
I shall forget fair Rosaline.'
"Her face is not as fair as mine!"
'And we shall blend a rich genetic mix
Which love to timeless rolling time shall fix.'

"But Romeo, what does one do
To make these coupled dreams come true?"
'Well Julie Love, I'm not sure yet —
Let's find out on the Internet —
Then veiled and clad in white from top to toe
You'll surely wed your loving Romeo.'

HEROES!

'Soap the stairs,' Macbeth decided,
'Then there'll only be a thud —
I might scratch myself with daggers,
And I loathe the sight of blood.'

'Comrades,' cried the brave King Harry,
'Even if they're still abed,
Send for gentlemen in England
So that they can fight instead.'

'Juliet,' replied her lover,
'I had better stay below —
Climbing balconies is dangerous,
Even though I love you so.'

'Peter,' said the star performer,
'Acting always takes its toll —
I'm so scared of too much roaring;
Could I have a smaller rôle?'

'Purnia,' whined mighty Caesar,
Constant as the Northern Star.
'On the Ides will it be raining?
Is the Senate very far?'

'Father,' cringed the dashing Hotspur,
'Henry's son is out to kill —
Couldn't I miss out on Shrewsbury?
P'r'aps I could be crafty ill.'

The Comedies

HEY NONNY NONNY

Lord Benedick of Padua,
A bachelor in root and stem,
Was loved by many ladies, though
He never had much time for them.

But Beatrice of Messina saw
No magic in his single charm,
And traded insults merrily
Without provoking much alarm.

Ensconced behind a tiny tree,
Lord Benedick hears planted words
Which speak of Beatrice's coy love.
And could this love be so absurd?

And hidden Beatrice hears her friends
Speak Benedick's enduring care,
And, pausingly, she thinks perhaps
There might be special bonding here.

The dashing Claudio soon falls
For Hero, daughter of the host,
For soldiers who are home on leave
Oft need the feminine the most.

Alas, bend-sinister Don John
Concocts a plan to falsely trawl
The rumour she's a wanton maid —
In fact she's not a maid at all.

The Constable and Headborough
Soon apprehend the soured Don John,
And through the Happy Wedded pair,
The spinning of the world goes on.

Reluctant Beatrice soon inflicts
Her matrimonial sympathy,
Because, says she, her Benedick's
Condition needs her empathy.

CADENCE

A liberator or a fool,
Jack Cade deplored the Grammar School
And also thought it was absurd
To think of words as noun or verb.

Fresh thinking men, who soon grow old,
Brought new ideas, so we were told;
Ideas originally displayed
By Holland, Bevis, Dick and Cade.

(Henry VI, Part 2, Act 4, Scene 7.)

BOYS

Rosalind and young Viola
Wore their manly clothes with poise
Like the offspring of Sir Rowland
Who were nominally boys.
What You Will and As You Like It
Bring us such confusing joys!

(See page 66)

A WINTER'S TALE

Leontes, King of southern Italy,
Unjustly thought Hermione, his Queen,
Was playing false with the Bohemian King,
Polixenes, whose childhood friend he'd been.

Polixenes fled home to foil a plot
To have him murdered with a hemlocked cup,
And as he flamed suspicion even more
Leontes had his pregnant Queen locked up.

The babe, by order of the deranged King,
Was left abandoned on a distant shore.
His son, a little like each king, expired,
Mourning his mother's lot and loneliness in store.

Named Perdita, because she had been lost,
A homespun shepherd found her on the strand,
Not guessing after sixteen nurtured years
A Prince would seek the fortune of her hand.

Polixenes, the father of the Prince,
Admired the comely maiden rather less,
His son was destined for a Stately Throne,
His Queen could never be a shepherdess.

Prince Florizel and Perdita took flight
To Sicily, to that Leontian shore;
And you, good Gentles, you should read the play,
If you wax warm and wish to know the more.

Repenting Leontes is slowly led
Into a chamber where the sculptors strive
To fashion stone into the living form —
A statue moves; and she is still alive.

RED AND WHITE

The garden of an Inn of Court
Was where the nobles proudly sought
To find supporters for their cause:
The starting of the Roses Wars.

A bishop long ago had warned
(Though at the time was roundly scorned)
That cousins swapping crown would bring
This time-delayed dynastic sting.

The prelate now should spend his life
Away from politics and strife,
Though Bolingbroke takes special care
To praise high honour he found there.

(Henry VI Part I, Act 2, Scene 4
Richard II, Act 4, Scene 1
Richard II, Act 5, Scene 6)

PERICLES

When Pericles returned from Antioch
Where he had found the incest of their king,
For safety of himself and of his realm
He was advised to take to travelling.

He sails for Tharsus and he helps relieve
The famine which that city's undergone,
But Antioch's assassin still pursues
And word from Tyre spells that he should move on.

He's shipwrecked on Pentapolis's shores,
But so excels there in his knightly skills
The King is pleased to pledge his daughter to
That troubled wandering man of unsought ills.

Recalled to Tyre, King Antiochus dead,
Amid confusion in a waveracked storm
His wife brings forth, though all think she has died,
A girl, Marina, who is safely born.

At Tharsus, left there in the governor's care,
She grew and soon began to overthrive,
While swooning mother, confined to the deep,
Was washed ashore, encasketed, alive!

Escaping carer's jealousy's cold knife,
And captured by a sharpened pirate band
The nubile maid is soon put up for sale
And purchased into rotting bawdyland.

Her beauties shine in grace and purity,
The clientele amazed, unsatisfied —
The governor, conquered by her quality,
Seeks out a way to have her bond untied.

Distraught and voiceless, thinking daughter dead,
He sips all known to audience — to us —
And, through a vision, he's Diana-led
To his lost wife, a priest at Ephesus.

FORD AND PAGE

Coveting their Windsor fortunes
With a bleary lustful eye
Falstaff dreams of sack and capons
At the Garter hostelry.

BEAR: ONE HEARS

'William,' moaned the shivering actor,
'This direction is unkind:
Winter is no time for exits,
Specially with a bear behind!'

SHREW

Bianca's suitors knew that they
Old bachelors would have to stay
Unless a husband should be found
To whom her sister could be bound —
But gentlemen, of course, all knew
Her sister was that dreadful Shrew.

Petruchio (né Richard Burton)
Felt he himself was almost certain
To conquer that pert renegade
For he, all knew, was Taylor-made.
(Bourgeoiserie, you understand,
Forbore to mention transferred land).

He would call Katherina, Kate,
He turned up for the nuptials late;
His wedding clothes were frayed and torn;
Enquickening hopes heirs might be born
He made it clear he'd no conception
Of staying on for the reception.

He scattered bedclothes on the floor,
And, *by mistake,* he slammed a door,
And when she dropped off in a doze
He tickled her half-frozen toes,
Pretending that her comfort lay
In kind concern, not disarray.

He almost gave her tasty food,
He said her newest gown was lewd,
And when it was the darkest night
He would insist the Sun shone bright —
Yet, Kiss me Kate, offsprung the dozens,
To join Bianca's lot, their cousins.

The children were a rowdy lot
Right from the day each left the cot —
The boys smashed everything in sight,
The girls wore lipstick far too bright,
But to their parents' fond relief
Their adolescences were brief.

Three husbands wagered it was they
Whose wife most fully would obey.
When summoned, one refused to come,
Another failed to join her chum;
So lords and masters felt like chumps
When Katherina turned up trumps.

A frosty tale, told thus in rime,
Is sure to melt if given time.
Two discords may, it has been shown,
Blend to a more harmonious tone —
For greying lovers, so it's said,
Enjoy their snuggles-up in bed.

With atoms of a different hue
The stronger bond between the two;
Magnetic poles of different sign
Will swing so that they soon align —
Each covered in pyjama'd fur
She keeps him warm, he comforts her;
They quarrel still, but not alone
For he is Darby, she is Joan.

LOVE'S LABOUR'S LOST

The King and three Lords of Navarre
Had sworn to banish comfort's snares
And never hear a woman's tongue
So they could study for three years,
Although it seemed they had not thought
What kind of knowledge would be sought.

All nubile, young and feminine
Four envoys from the King of France
Were welcomed by the forsworn Lords,
They having booked well in advance;
But each with each, like hand in glove,
Soon fell, quite hopelessly, in love.

Berowne, the talker of the four,
Although the other three were loth,
Explains how academe demands
The breaking of their solemn oath.
(Playgoers lost in verbal tricks
Just wonder if it's all a fix).

When all is merry and afling,
A message from the ladies' court
Truncates the carefree jollity —
Their agued King, alas, is mort —
Though that's for those whose French is poor,
One really says: *Le Roi est mort.*

Each gave her swain a heavy task,
And if each to his task were true,
Then after twelve months and a day
Each would be free to love and woo.
Those merriments no more than foam,
Each lady now must soon go home.

As owl and cuckoo make their song,
To end this not-so-simple play,
This would-be Shakespeare, so he dreams,
Awards himself the final say:
Good Gentles, who take such an oath
Choose love or learning, never both.

SPRING

When daisies pied and violets blue
And lady-smocks all silver-white
And cuckoo buds of yellow hue
Do paint the meadows with delight,
The cuckoo then on every tree
Mocks married men, for thus sings he:
'Cuckoo;
Cuckoo, cuckoo' — O word of fear,
Unpleasing to a married ear!

WINTER

When icicles hang by the wall
And Dick the shepherd blows his nail,
And Tom bears logs into the hall,
And milk comes frozen home in pail,
When blood is nipp'd, and ways be foul,
Then nightly sings the staring owl:
'Tu-who;
Tu-whit, tu-who' — A merry note,
While greasy Joan doth keel the pot.

William Shakespeare

THE STORM

Dusty tomes and cobwebbed studies
May have warranted rebuke
In the city of Milano,
Where, of course, I was the Duke.

When my brother had me ousted
Though my future hopes were low
I retained my little daughter
And that buffoon Trinculo.

Settling on this tiny island
I acquired a misformed slave,
And a helpful little spirit
Caught up in a cloven stave.

Caliban, the first aforesaid,
Kept locked up for all our sakes,
Didn't take to education
So I rack him with old aches.

When a ship conveying nobles
Satisfied star-wandering lore
Magic which I had concocted
Forced them all to come ashore.

One would suit my dear Miranda —
He's the King of Naples' son.
One's Antonio, my brother,
From whose greed these troubles sprung.

Soon two happy plighted lovers
Are discovered playing chess;
Stephano goes off imbibing,
Caliban clears up the mess.

Daddy, said the fair Miranda,
Now we're going to Milan,
Will the others be like Ferdy
Or like poor old Caliban?

ADDENDUM

Prospero gets back his Dukedom;
Faithful Ariel's set free;
Sundry nobles are forgiven;
Magic then recalms the sea.

TWO GENTLEMEN

Romeo and Juliet,
Montague and Capulet
At Verona might have met
With those two good friends of mine,
Proteus and Valentine.

In reverse the same is true:
Capulet and Montague
At Verona might renew
With those two good friends of us,
Valentine and Proteus.

CASKETS

Bassanio had lived in style
And owed Antonio a pile
But thought that if he borrowed more
Then somehow he might square the score.

He knew a lady, pure and staid,
(Whose father's fortune had been made) —
Yes, Portia was a gradely lass;
But to court her he would need brass.

The banks were such a stingy bunch
You'd think they owned the Credit Crunch —
They wouldn't lend a ducat to
A man whose sureties were few.

At length a three-month loan was gained
The terms of which were grossly stained;
Default would mean that human heart
And flesh around would have to part.

His threadbare jeans would have to go,
And hand-made suits from Saville Row
Would grace portmanteaux which would bear
Initialled silken underwear,

He'd do what pukka nobles do.
He'd boast about a Duke or two,
And to enrich his bluest lie
He'd wear an Old Etonian tie.

Three caskets, silver, lead and gold,
But only one of them would hold
The portrait which needs must decide
The right to claim her as a bride.

Some minor suitors for her hand
Chose wrongly, just as she had planned —
Too grim, too grum, too fat, too old:
Some chose silver, others gold.

She had a trimetallic key
Which left her clandestinely free
To move the caskets' contents where
Bassanio could find them there.

But when she realised what he'd spent,
How much old Shylock must have lent,
She felt that she was losing track
Of how much Muggins must pay back.

Fair Portia was the legal star,
Though never summoned to the bar,
Who helped Antonio procure
Annulment of his forfeiture.

Read on, good Gentles, what is writ:
This drama's greatest hypocrite
Sneers at the riches of the Jew,
Then steals his cash and daughter too;

And what perhaps is even worse,
He lards his crime with starlit verse,
With stanzas which as they unfold
Are vainly speckled with his gold.

ANTIPHOLUS

Egeon who had searched the world —
Five empty years at sea —
At length arrives at Ephesus
To seek his family.

Illegal entry usually
Involved a hefty fine,
With execution following
If it's not paid on time.

Antipholus, Antipholus,
Each the other's twin;
With Dromio and Dromio
Thus also born akin.

Antipholus and Dromio
Had never caused much fuss
Before this Comedy began
At peaceful Ephesus.

Antipholus and Dromio
Arrived from Syracuse
Which was the perfect recipe
To muddle and confuse.

Egeon, the old traveller,
Was certainly most glad
When each of the Antipholoi
Turned out to be his lad.

Not only that, Egeon found
The Abbess was his wife;
Good Gentles, p'r'aps you don't believe
Such things go on in life.

Enantiomers

ALL'S WELL THAT ENDS WELL

A clever doctor's daughter, Helena,
Brought up at Bertram's (Count Roussillon's) Court,
Is in the Dowager's especial care
While strangled dreams dare scarce give love a thought.

Prescriptions from her father's dying hand
Hold promise of extraordinary cure,
So Helena brings France's King a hope
While his physicians offer but despair.

If he is healed, she will fulfil a wish:
To choose the man to whom she will be wed —
Rejecting all the flower of Paris youth,
She chooses Bertram, as she planned, instead.

The Count is loath to take her eager hand,
But out of duty to his aged King,
He marries her but will not go abed;
And sips what fortune foreign war may bring.

He will not take her truly as his wife
Unless she is the mother of his child,
And not until the ring he always wears
Can from his clinging finger be beguiled.

Pretending to be Bertram's chosen love,
She visits in the greyness of the night;
And you, fair matrons, do you blench in shock,
Or do you think it was her nuptial right?

As Helena fulfilled her twofold task
The Count relents and takes her for his wife,
As pressured men may well do, given time
To weigh the fortune-balanced scales of life.

NELL

'Pistol,' said the red-nosed Bardolph,
'If you've set your heart on Nell,
You had better marry Quickly —
Nym is after her as well.'

GLASS OF FASHION

'Hamlet,' said the cross Ophelia,
'Are these clothes to be your norm?
Once you were the glass of fashion,
Now you are the mould of scorn.'

WINTER'S CALL

When temperatures begin to fall,
And logs are switched on in the hall,
And everyone is milky pale
And Dick sighs blow to more junk mail;
An owl complains, in curious hoot,
Transmitted by a devious route:
Ting-ling, ting-ling — a merry note,
Learnt from the mobile phone, by rote.

MEASURE FOR MEASURE

The Duke, a kind and modest man,
Retired from duty for a span;
He'd say that he was far away,
Though, in disguise, he planned to stay.

Helped by a veritable sage,
Encrusted with excessive age,
Lord Angelo was left behind
With duties that were ill-defined.

He very soon revived a law
Which gave the dreaded sentence for
A man who led a maid astray
Before her lawful wedding day.

Now Juliet had been beguiled
By Claudio, and had a child,
A fault which he could not deny,
So he was thus about to die.

His sister, destined for the veil,
Was brought the news of his travail
And pushed aside all else to go
To plead with cold Lord Angelo.

At first her arguments were vain,
For Angelo had made it plain
That nothing she could do or say
Would save her brother's life next day.

But Angelo was weakened man,
And presently proposed a plan:
Her brother's pardon could be bought
By sister's yielding all he sought.

Her brother pleaded for his life —
She answered like a sharpened knife:
She thought it better he should die
Than her chaste purity should lie.

A jilted lady made the tryst
So that the sister wasn't missed.
Though Angelo was easily fooled,
His taste for mercy quickly cooled.

By using a dead pirate's head
It seemed that Claudio was dead,
And though this play is much contrived,
All, but the pirate, had survived.

The Duke, returning, took great pride
In matching man with rightful bride,
Though in his final words inferred
A union which seemed quite absurd.

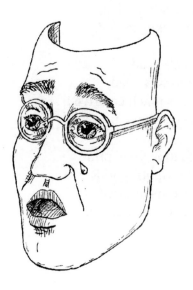

The Histories
and
The Roman Plays

KING JOHN

Yes, John, de facto, was the king,
As minstrelsy would no doubt sing,
But primogeniture decreed
That Geffrey's boy should first succeed.
(Another sprang from Richard's fount,
But bastards never really count) —
Good matrons should take better care
Concerning VIPs they bear,
For then there would be lesser need
For countless wounded men to bleed.

The worried John made quick repair
To try to capture Angiers,
But that walled town refused to yield
Until it knew who held the field —
Did Philip, King of France, hold sway
Or would things swing the other way?
Would Geffrey's widow, for her son,
Soon win a throne to sit upon?
And Elinor, how had she viewed
This sordid blood-stained family feud?

The warring parties soon made peace
By joining Louis to John's niece,
(The lady, Blanche, one must explain
Had gone with John on his campaign) —
The boy she had to take on board,
The cream of France, their foremost lord,
Was thoughtless, vain, and prone to spout,
And yet she had to wed the lout.
Fair princesses, when apt to roam,
Should settle down and stay at home.

The senseless war had been rejoined
Before the pair were quite enloined,
For peace would mean King Philip went
Where John already had been sent — *
And so it comes as no surprise
John sought to burn his rival's eyes,
Which filled his cronies with disgust,
Eroding all baronial trust;
And when he had himself recrowned
The Council Tax went up a pound.

When John, from overeating, died,
And only crocodiles had cried,
At home the barons subtly thought
What Henry Three should now be taught:
Perhaps, planned they, if given time,
They'd found a new de Montfort line.
The Franks, abroad, shrugged, '*Il est bon,*
We never liked that *rosbif Jean.*'
To Worcester Jean was taken, where
A box containing him's still there.

I really think I should display
What Shakespeare quite forgot to say:
The English race was partly freed
By what John signed at Runnymede,
Though charters pledged with due duress
Need time to germinate success.
And yes, it isn't fully tosh
His crown went missing in the Wash;
But if you think King John a fool
It's he who founded Liverpool!

* King John had been excommunicated, and King Philip had been
threatened with excommunication.

RICHARD II

The monarch of this Sceptred Isle
Had ruled in somewhat devious style
While flatterers smeared on esteem —
Like Bushy, Bagot, Wiltshire, Green —
And though he'd sorted out those peasants
His realm was green, but far from pleasant.

Now Norfolk had done Gloucester down
On orders coming from the Crown,
And Bolingbroke, that honest lad,
Had found that Norfolk was the cad.
Richard, of course, hoped none should know it,
But thought that Bolingbroke might blow it.

The worried King thus banished both
And made the twain each take an oath
Lest they in exile bargains made,
And, joined in hate, might soon invade.
When Bolingbroke's old dad lay dying
He didn't waste much time in crying —

He grabbed old John of Gaunt's estate,
His land, his revenues, his plate,
By confiscating on the spot
All that his first-born should have got.
Though when he issued those blank charters
He changed tax-payers into martyrs.

Since he had overseas concerns —
Pursuing those rough-headed kerns —
He left his uncle York in charge
(A task that he found far too large),
And sailed across St George's Channel,
His soldiers decked in paid for flannel.

As soon as Bolingbroke returned —
From Brittany it soon was learned —
One heard all bards and minstrels sing
That he would make a better king —
Thus House of Lancaster was started;
And Yorkists schemed and soured and smarted.

FALSTAFF

'Falstaff,' quipped the heir apparent,
'When I've won my progress prize,
You and Bardolph, Poins and Peto
Should expect a big surprise.'

'Gone the carefree days at Eastcheap
When Prince Hal would call me Jack;
Now, alas, I am rejected,
Though I'm pleased I got the *sack!'*

MINOR POET

Some clever academic said
That rhyme, of course, is stony dead,
And scansion too, since I have found
Without it I am more profound —
Had Shakespeare only understood
He really might have been quite good.

KING DICK

Bolingbroke and Thomas Mowbray
Each felt they had served the King —
Each was banished for his loyalty
Lest they disclose everything.

'Bagot,' moaned the lonely Richard,
'You are held in great esteem,
But our other friends are missing:
Where is Bushy? Where is Green?'

'Inky blots and rotten parchments
Have farmed out my realm it's true,
But my issue of blank charters
Never has been, will be, new.'

'Mortimer,' joked Harry Hotspur,
'Shall we call Glendower's bluff?
— Lovely well he calls up spirits,
And there's all that fiery stuff!'

Though Carlisle told turncoat nobles
Bolingbroke should not be king,
Henry saw that opposition
Could from sparks of honour spring.

Duke and Duchess found high treason
In their little-county son,
He denounced him, she redeemed him,
Bringing endless groundling fun.

Teeming nothingness; each day is
Crawling, flitting into ten;
Richard sits in Pomfret Castle
Waiting for his Cousin's Men.

Jewelled and Golden is the Orbis,
Seeming fount of Majesty,
Warranty for neither Kingship
Nor for immortality.

INSPECTION

All generals know that they should smile
At officers **and** rank and file,
And eve of battle should be spent
On visiting each soldier's tent.
When Henry's sternest calling spoke
He borrowed Erpingham's old cloak,
So grey and plain it did not bear
The stamp of kingship in its wear.
Tom's archers' volleys make all blench
When aimed at the advancing French;
But I'll advance my daring ploy
By saying that I'm called Le Roy,
And monitor each nod and wink
To find out what my troopers think
And boost the courage they'll display
At Agincourt, on Crispin's Day.

HENRY V

The bishops thought that 'as things stand
The Crown might confiscate our land';
So they encouraged war abroad
So that the exploits of the sword
Would keep the King's ambitions warm
And take his mind off land reform.

The foolish Dauphin brashly galls
The King by sending tennis balls,
Pretending, in some devilish measure,
That he had sent a ton of treasure,
Expecting doubtlessly to score
Some credit for provoking war.

When ready to embark for France,
The fight took on a different stance:
A disappointed King found reason
To execute three men for treason —
Cambridge and Grey were of that group,
But, worst of all, there was Lord Scroop.

The brave Fluellen often bores
With tales of disciplines of wars;
Macmorris shows the Irish kern
Will little change as centuries turn,
While Captain James and Captain Gower
Spell Scottish thistle, English flower.

Harfleur surrendered when they knew
All that the English troops might do —
What joy for wives, what hope for child
When battle-hardened men run wild?
When King, and army, marched for home
He urged that mercy should be shown.

When Bardolph who had been a pal,
And might have even called him Hal,
Was hanged for sacrilege and theft
The King showed scorn for all he'd left —
For Nym and Poins and gross Sir John —
His Cheapside life — so quickly gone.

French notables began to stir
On hearing that they'd lost Harfleur —
And planned to fight at Agincourt —
Indeed, what were they waiting for?
The English, though now sick and few,
Still aimed to show what they could do.

The Frenchmen did not care to know
The strength of England's yeomen's bow,
So soon, their ranks in disarray,
The flowers of France were plucked away,
While England triumphed, so it's said,
With only five and twenty dead.

Though Henry's French was none too good
He made it clear just where he stood —
The Princess Kate would be his bride,
Of this he would not be denied;
So when their loins brought forth a son
Then France and England would be one.

HENRY VI Part III

The Yorkists break into the parliament
And Richard boldly takes the regal Throne,
And though King Henry feels his claims are weak
It's not a view supporters could condone.

Both Richard and King Henry take an Oath,
Agreeing Henry will retain the Crown
But when he dies then Richard will be King
While Henry's heir, Prince Edward, will stand down.

The Queen, enraged, soon marches off to war
And slaughters Edmund, Richard's tutored son,
And as his captured father waits to die
Her taunts bring her backtwisted-evil fun.

Near Hereford three glorious suns are seen —
Perhaps they signify the brothers who
Will be uplifted into Yorkist kings —
Three suns there were, but only seen by two.

Warwick and war decide who shall be King,
Who bears that orb as hourglass grains ill-run,
So Edward, fourth to clasp the sceptred rod,
Succeeds the fruit of John of Gaunt's fourth son.

Warwick, no doubt, should chose the King's fair bride
And makes to France to treat for her royal hand;
While Edward stays at home and quietly woos
A widow who has sadly lost her land.

The French King raves, the Earl of Warwick too
When it leaks out the Monarch's wed by stealth;
The Queen still hopes, for husband and for son,
Unlike poor Bona, left upon the shelf.

The hunchback Gloucester with his withered arm
Who cannot charm a lady's gentle care,
With many heads between him and the Crown,
Thinks of the bloodshed that can lead him there.

Poor Henry's murdered, a good decent man,
But, such is life, he wasn't greatly missed,
The Yorkist flower blooms on an extra day;
And Gloucester ticks another on his list.

RICHARD III

When Gloucester marries Anne, although
He'd killed her husband and his father,
She no doubt lies awake all night,
Her nightgown drenched in fear-chilled lather.

Two ruffians are hired to kill
The Duke of Clarence, Gloucester's brother;
One stabs and takes the rotten gold,
While conscience wins the thoughtful other.

The dying Edward seeks a truce
Between those nobles who are newer
And those of older family stem
Whose blood may seem a whole lot bluer.

A truce, of course, that is embraced
By good avuncular old Gloucester,
But heads he chops when Edward dies
Soon show him as the great imposter.

Prince Edward, Edward's son, now King,
And Richard Duke of York, his brother,
Are lured into the murderous Tower
While ears of fear surround their mother.

And Buckingham, with googly spin,
In charge of Gloucester's propaganda,
Soon lost his head without, forsooth,
His Richard-promised rich backhander.

So Richard rules, for two years king,
And history turns its blacker pages,
Till Henry, thirsting power, invades
And Bosworth ends the Middle Ages.

But there are some who climb the tree
To power-crazed Downing Number-tenner,
Who murder truth so they can be
A Hackster or a Matchwood-Jenner —
Like Richard, Gentles, they, of course,
Will soon go tumbling from their horse.

JULIUS

'Cassius,' said mighty Caesar,
'Do we have to be so bold —
Tiber bathing's rather risky
And I'm sure to catch a cold.'

'Julius,' said cross Calpurnia,
'If they offer you that crown,
I'm the one who'll have to clean it —
Why not turn the darned thing down?'

DOCTOR

With a drying sticky wicket,
With spectators wearing thin,
Buckingham, the Duke's own captain,
Feels that he should bring on spin.

(Richard III, Act 3, Scene 7)

HENRY VIII

When Henry gatecrashed Wolsey's do
He found a pretty face or two,
But, to be fair, he didn't plan
To seek his wife's attendant, Anne.

Although he thought she might be fun
He urgently required a son,
Because there was residual talk
Of rivals from the House of York.

Since Katharine could not produce
She really wasn't any use,
So he devised a devious course
To gain annulment or divorce.

For she had previously been wed,
Though p'r'aps she hadn't shared his bed,
To Henry's brother, Arthur, who
Had been the elder of the two.

Because she'd been his brother's wife —
That meant the partner of his life
Had not brought forth that healthy boy
Who would have been his father's joy.

The Vatican was not impressed
By what he claimed to be incest,
And so, to ease his path at home,
The ageing King then broke with Rome.

Queen Anne, for soon she was to be,
Did not extend the family tree —
Her pregnancy set all awhirl,
But then the baby was a girl.

She got the chop and he felt free
To marry Jane, his number three —
She died in giving him an heir,
And I will end the story there.

Good Queens who share a regal bed,
Keep very calm, don't lose your head,
And most importantly don't fail
To have some babies who are male.

Just give your king a friendly hug,
And give your forelock a nice tug,
And ask him to remove his crown
Before you turn and snuggle down.

REGIME CHANGE

The King was bitten by a snake,
Although, they say, that tale's a fake;
The Prince, 'tis true, went off his head
And two schoolfriends of his are dead;
It's curtains for our Chamberlain —
And no-one's willing to explain.

His daughter too may have mistook
The meaning in young Hamlet's look;
And now, if what they say is true,
Some young Norwegian parvenu
Invaded with a well-armed band
And wants to rule our crazy land.

Election Day at Elsinore —
Who will the Danes be voting for?
Now that their day of Royalty's spent
They're looking for a President,
Since no-one would be quite so crass
As choose usurping Fortinbras.

Redundant courtiers might stand,
Like Osric or like Voltimand:
Such candidates would blithely prate,
'There's something rotten in the State,'
And try to woo the People's heart
With less of matter, more of art.

A President — well that's a thought —
For they're no better than they ought —
Might they not *know-not* Gertrude's *seems*
With policies composed of dreams,
And as they gild what lies in store
How much will change at Elsinore?

TIP OF TONGUE

'Where, oh curse it?' spluttered Hotspur,
'Did I yield my supple knee
To that Bolingbroke usurper —
In Gloucestershire —
It starts with B.

Answer on page 66

CAIUS MARCIUS

Volumnia had always thought
That Roman honour could be bought
Through her Marstrained intrepid son
And all the victories he had won.

Unlike Virgilia, his wife,
Who lived a sew-sew indoor life,
He relished the Volscian War
So he could knock on Honour's door.

His exploits brought so wide a fame
They granted him an extra name;
So that the Bard could entertain us
With his play, *Coriolanus.*

Their Tribunes banished him from Rome
And Corioli was his home,
Since he was such a dreadful snob
And hated the plebeian mob.

Aufidius, his latter foe,
Was pleased at where he chose to go,
And let him lead the army back
So Rome itself was facing sack.

His aged mother, son and wife
All pleaded for the city's life,
So what could he now think or say
That wasn't shaded medium grey?

The treaty that his mother sought
Belied the essence of her thought,
And as his will began to bend
He knew his life was at an end.

'Tell me, Conscience,' whispered Henry,
'Tell me truly if you can.
Was I really wed to Katherine?
Was it just I wanted Anne?'

'Think Lorenzo,' whispered conscience,
'Think about your Christian life —
You are fond of Jewish ducats
And would have a Jewish wife.'

JULIUS CAESAR

'On the Lupercal,' schemed Caesar,
'I won't seek out kingship yet —
I will thrice refuse the offer
So it seems I'm hard to get.'

'Cassius,' thought wily Caesar,
'Bears a lean and hungry look;
Give me men who love their comforts,
Men that I can bring to book.'

'Ah Calpurnia,' smiled Caesar,
'We're a noble Roman pair —
Hodie Rex Romanorum —
You shall be the Queen, My Dear.'

'Signs and portents presage danger;
Tell the Senate he is sick.'
'Caesar is above suspicion. —
He would never play a trick!'

'Caesar,' cried Artemidorus,
'On this paper are the names
Of such men who would destroy you —
All but one with selfish aims.'

'Et tu Brute!' whispered Caesar,
'What betrayal friendship hides;
Augurers forbade me venture
From my house upon the Ides.'

Shakespeare's father, John, was a glover, and was probably illiterate. However he became an alderman and High Bailiff (equivalent to Mayor) of Stratford-upon-Avon.

Although Shakespeare was a rich man in later life, he left his wife, Anne, only his second-best bed.

Restaurants in Stratford are Barred from serving Bacon!

EAUX DE NIL

When Cleopatra ruled this land
With pyramids, though mostly sand,
A Roman general came to stay
And no doubt had his wicked way;

Though married he set her on fire
*Mark*ed as the man she could admire,
While she, no doubt, had really meant
To open their new parliament.

So when her lord sailed back to Rome
To deal with brewing plots at home,
And then she heard he had re-wed
The pampered Queen, of course, saw red.

But longing lingered all the while
Just like the ever flowing Nile,
Enriched, as some may understand,
By ichor from a distant land.

But how did starlit lovers speak:
Maybe in Latin, maybe Greek —
And when the pair began to hanker
They doubtless spoke a lingua franca.

Defeated Anthony's misled
In thinking Cleopatra dead,
And knows the triumph Caesar scored
Must mean his falling on his sword.

Mistrusting their new Master's plans —
The jeering of Plebeian fans —
The Queen and Ladies choose to die
Not knowing where the truth may lie!

Q Q Q Q

More should I question thee, and more I must.
(All's well that ends well, Act 2 Scene 1)

QUIZ

1. Why did the waking Juliet
    Call Romeo a churl?
2. And then, to crown the tragedy,
    How did the plot unfurl?

3. Which shaking facial weakness did
    Sir Andrew's cheek proclaim
4. And which vulgarity was shown
    Within Sir Toby's name?

5. Who went to fight rug-headed kerns
    That lived beyond the Pale?
6. And what did Chuck say he should do
    So that they wouldn't fail?

7. Whose ducal bonnet was removed
    To greet an oyster wench?
8. Which 'silent' shallow justices
    Sat on a country bench?

9. When icicles hung by the wall
    Which lady keeled the pot?
10. Which English king was crowned abroad
    When but a tiny tot?

11. When Troilus fell for Cressida
    Where did the lovers meet?
12. What can't you do by thinking on
    Fantastic summer's heat?

13. What did the Lordly gentleman
    Hold in his scented hand?
14. Where did the smug and silver Trent
    Rob Hotspur of his land?

15. Which colour did Olivia
    Allegedly abhor?
16. Which Captain, with his disciplines,
    Was apt to be a bore?

17. Who thrice refused, though craftily,
    A proffered kingly crown?
18. Whose bucket rose to majesty
    As Richard's pail went down?

19. Which bard was born in Warwickshire
    Upon Saint George's Day?
20. And what did shake the darling buds
    When it was only May?

21. Who were the ghosts that Richard saw
    The night before he died?
22. And to which very Roman wife
    Was noble Brutus tied?

23. Which knighted, pontooned bird of prey
    Was aide-de-camp to John?
24. And who reminded Caesar that
    The Ides had not yet gone?

And, the following quatrain requires four answers:

25. ' Octavian,' said Antony
    'Shouldn't we be three
    Just like the old Triumvirate
    Of C. and C. and P. ?

Answers on Page 66

Across: 1. Jointed limbs for simple constable (6)
        5. Twin servant (6)

Down: 1. Richard's father and grandfather (6)
        2. Ancestor to many monarchs (6)
        3. Of all to Caesar (6)
        4. Island poet in Sonnet 38 (6)

The crossword involves no other words.

Solution on Page 67

BOTTOM LINE

R.S.C. and R.S.C. are unidentical twins — The Royal
Shakespeare Company and the Royal Society of Chemistry.
Each was interested when a fragrance company, Quest
International, attempted to produce the potion which led to
Titania, the Queen of the Fairies, accidentally falling in love
with Bottom, an extrovert weaver, who had somehow
acquired an ass's head. The aphrodisiac had a scent described
as heady and sweet, and like Parma violets. Guidance was
found in Act 2 Scene 1 of *A Midsummer-Night's Dream*,
where the necessary components, described by the King of the
Fairies, were rapidly gathered by the industrious Robin
Goodfellow.

> *Yet marked I where the bolt of Cupid fell.*
> *It fell upon a little western flower*

Virtually no chemistry was known in Shakespearean times,
and pharmacy was primitive. However, the words *distilled*
and *tincture* do occur in the plays.

QUIZ ANSWERS

Page 55:   Berkeley Castle

Pages 62 / 63
1. He had left no poison for her.
2. Juliet stabbed herself.
3. Ague.
4. Belch.
5. Richard II.
6. Screw his courage to the sticking place.
7. Bolingbroke.
8. Robert Shallow and Silence.
9. Greasy Joan.
10. Henry VI.
11. Pandarus's orchard in Troy.
12. Wallow naked in December snow.
13. A pouncet-box.
14. Near Burton-on-Trent.
15. Yellow.
16. Fluellen.
17. Julius Caesar.
18. Bolingbroke.
19. William Shakespeare.
20. Rough winds.
21. All the people he had killed.
22. Portia.
23. Philip Faulconbridge, who became Sir Philip
    Plantagenet.
24. A soothsayer.
25. Lepidus. Julius Caesar, Crassus, and Pompey.

Page 19:   Offspring of Sir Rowland de Boys.

CROSSWORD SOLUTION

E	L	B	O	W	S
D		A	M		A
W		N	N		P
A		Q	I		P
R		U	U		H
D	R	O	M	I	O

The Real Thing

SONNET 29

When in disgrace with Fortune and men's eyes,
I all alone beweep my outcast state,
And trouble deaf heaven with my bootless cries,
And look upon myself, and curse my fate,
Wishing me like to one more rich in hope,
Featured like him, like him with friends
possessed,
Desiring this man's art, and that man's scope,
With what I most enjoy contented least;
Yet in these thoughts myself almost despising,
Haply I think on thee, and then my state,
Like to the lark at break of day arising
From sullen earth, sings hymns at heaven's gate;
For thy sweet love remembered such wealth
brings
That then I scorn to change my state with kings.

Lightning Source UK Ltd.
Milton Keynes UK
12 November 2010

162783UK00008B/95/P